PILGRIM IN ADVENT

Donal Neary SJ

Pilgrim
in
Advent

the columba press

First published in 1994 by
the columba press
93 The Rise, Mount Merrion,
Blackrock, Co Dublin

Cover by Bill Bolger
Origination by The Columba Press
Printed in Ireland by
Genprint Ltd, Dublin

ISBN 1 85607 116 2

Acknowledgements

Bloodaxe Books for Brendan Kennelly, *A Giving;* The Catholic
Herald for Ronald Rolheiser, *Give Comfort to My People;* Fontana
Books for Teilhard de Chardin, *The Divine Milieu;* Darton,
Longman and Todd for Sheila Cassidy, *Light from the Dark
Valley;* Doctrine and Life, for Dermot Lane, *In Search of Hope;*
Fount Books, for Kathleen O'Sullivan, *Light Out of Darkness;*
The Goldsmith Press, for Patrick Kavanagh, *Collected Poems;*
Paulist Press for L Patrick Carroll and Katherine Dyckman,
Chaos or Creation; The Columba Press for Donal O'Leary, *Windows
of Wonder;* The Independent, for Janet Martin Soskice; Words-
worth Poetry Library for W B Yeats, *A Prayer for my Son* and
The Magi.

All unacknowledged Reflections are by the author.

Contents

Introduction

Pilgrim in Advent is a preparation in prayer for the feast of Christmas. Taking as its themes Wilderness, Change, Witness and Birth – four principal themes or images of Advent – *Pilgrim in Advent* offers prayers, Scripture and Reflections to help us on our prayer-journey to Christmas.

How to use Pilgrim in Advent

Choose a time and a place for your daily prayer. A time when you will not be disturbed, and a place where you will be sure of some quiet and little interruption is best: like in your room, or a church, or somewhere you can get quiet from others and noise. One person used pray in the car in the garage as the only place for quiet from the young family!

Choose a time when you are less harassed than others, when you are not tired and can put the ordinary cares and jobs away. First thing in the morning or last thing at night can be good times, or just before a meal. The middle of the day can be a good time to snatch a few minutes, even in a quiet place during a lunch-break.

Find the amount of time you like yourself. Try to stick to the amount of time you have decided – 10, 15 minutes, or what-ever time you choose and are comfortable with. You need enough time for the words to sink in and to allow some depth in your contact with the Lord, but not taking on so much that you will be bored and tempted to give up.

You need not cover all the material. Sometimes you might

like to read through it and go back to what strikes you as significant for a certain day. This may be from any of the pieces of the day. In prayer the Lord has a particular message or word for you each day. On the seventh day of each week, you might like to repeat one of the day' themes which you found meant a lot to you.

Reading the scripture or other material aloud can be a way of allowing it reach you in depth. There is no hurry to move on. If an image or idea brings you into prayer, stay there.

Pilgrim in Advent is based on four Advent themes or images. The first week introduces us to the wilderness, the place associated with John the Baptist as he prepared to announce the Lord, and also with the Lord Jesus' own preparation for his ministry. The themes in this week are from the 'wilderness experiences' of our lives, and finding the word of God which expresses and heals these experiences.

Repentance or change is another big theme of Advent and is the theme of the second week. These readings and prayers invite and challenge us to deep changes in our lives as we prepare for the coming of Christ.

Our third week introduces us to witnesses of Advent – people who were witnesses of the birth of Christ, each in a unique way inviting us to be witnesses ourselves like them.

In the fourth week, we allow the strong image of birth be our entry-point to prayer, as we pray over ways in which God comes to birth, like Jesus did, in our world today through us.

Pilgrim in Advent may also be used in groups. Some parishes use it for daily advent prayer, in the morning or the evening, adapting it accordingly and adding some music. Schools may find it helpful for Assemblies or varied forms of Advent prayer.

The first week of Advent

Wilderness

1.1 Lost in the wilderness

INTRODUCTION Feeling lost in life is a type of 'spiritual wilderness' – the loss of love, of health, of home, of meaning in life. As you can get lost in a wilderness and a desert, you can get lost for a time in life. What will give direction to you?

SCRIPTURE *Jesus goes out to look for the lost.*
Then Jesus went about all the cities and villages, teaching in their synagogues, and proclaiming the good news of the kingdom, and curing every disease and sickness. When he saw the crowds, he had compassion on them, because they were harrassed and helpless, like sheep without a shepherd. Then he said to his disciples, 'The harvest is plentiful, but the labourers are few; therefore ask the Lord of the harvest to send out labourers into his harvest.' *Matthew 9:35-38.*

PSALM
Incline your ear, O Lord, and answer me,
for I am poor and needy.
Preserve my life, for I am devoted to you;
save your servant who trusts in you.
You are my God; be gracious to me, O Lord,
for to you do I cry all day long. *Psalm 86.*

PRAYER
Lost but finding our way –
this is a real and frequent human experience:
lost in failure and bereavement,
lost in confusion and worry,
lost in loneliness and self-hatred;

looking for a safe hand or a confident word,
like the child lost in the city,
the young adult lost in confusion about the future,
or the old person lost in memory of the long-past.

Come, Lord Jesus,
come and look for those you love;
come with the gentleness of God,
the hand that never goes cold,
the word that is always new.

Come, Lord Jesus,
onto the pathway,
through the fog,
out of the darkness,

come, Lord Jesus,
way of God,
light of God,
brightness of God.

REFLECTION
The follower of Jesus Christ is never lost. All of our lives we
want to be found; we want meaning in life, a doorway to
truth, a love that will last; we want something that will make
sense of our past and give roots to our future. This we find in
Jesus, for he is the meaning of life, the truth that never fades,
the love that flows through every year of our lives. I think
'Rock' is a strong word, but not the best image for Jesus. I pre-
fer 'Flow'. He is the grace that flows through every experience we have: through every love and loss, every failure and
friendship, every heartache and happiness. We may feel lost,
but not forever. In Advent we wait, not as people lost and
ignorant of being saved, but waiting in patience, certainty
and in sure hope that God is near.

INTRODUCTION We search in our lives for God. We know that we are incomplete. Because Jesus, the child of God, is carried on his journey to birth, we know our search is not in vain; that we are carried by God in our searching.

SCRIPTURE *The search for acceptance and love in the woman at the well of Jacob is over: she has met Jesus and has reached the goal of her searching in him.*

Jesus said, 'If you knew the gift of God and who it is that is saying to you, 'Give me a drink', you would have asked him and he would have given you living water.' The woman said to him, 'Where do you get that living water?' Jesus said to her, 'Everyone who drinks of this water will be thirsty again, but those who drink of the water that I will give them will never be thirsty.' *John 4:10-14.*

PSALM
O God you are my God, I seek you,
my soul thirsts for you; my flesh faints for you,
as in a dry weary land where there is no water. *Psalm 63.*

PRAYER
Where is God?
a question asked in silence,
or in the signs and words of the heart.

We search for God,
for the centre of our being,
for the love which ever fails,

for peace in times of prayer:
ways we know God is near.

God is near.
For the woman looking for water,
God was the tired man at the well.
When our search for God is too complicated,
we may miss him close at hand.

He is in you and in me;
he is the love between two people;
he is the flow of life that enlivens our distress
and the spark of hope that enlightens our darkness.

He is in the word of sympathy,
the concern for employment and shelter,
the work for food and education.

In the searching is the finding,
and that is why Jesus says,
'If you seek, you will always find.'

And when you find God,
it's something like the Bethlehem journey:
God has been travelling for you,
searching for you.

Child of the search,
searching for birth and home,
like all of us seeking
a place to belong, a place of welcome,
be with us in our searching.

REFLECTION
I thank you, my God, for having in a thousand different
ways led my eyes to discover the immense simplicity of
things. Little by little, through the irresistible development

13

of those yearnings you implanted in me as a child, through the influence of gifted friends who entered my life at certain moments to bring light and strength to my mind, and through the awakenings of spirit I owe to the successive initiations, gentle and terrible, which you caused me to undergo: through all these I have been brought to the point where I can no longer see anything, nor any longer breathe, outside that milieu in which all is made one.

Teilhard de Chardin, *The Divine Milieu.*

1.3   The wilderness of disappointment

INTRODUCTION In the disappointments we experience, we find ourselves like being in a wilderness; disappointments, for example, in a relationship, in study, health, employment, promotion, or any of the disillusionments of life.

SCRIPTURE *Behind this simple statement in the gospel lies the disappointment of many years for a couple who had no children.*

Elizabeth and Zechariah had no children, because Elizabeth was barren, and both were getting on in years. *Luke 1:7.*

PSALM
You, O Lord, are my lamp,
my God who lightens my darkness.
With you I can break through any barrier,
with my God I can scale any wall. *Psalm 17.*

PRAYER
They had hoped for many years to have a child;
a good husband and wife,
people who took religion seriously
and prayed to their God.

How much disappointment was in their lives?
The years of hoping and bitterness,
the years of accepting and blaming,
the years of longing and loving.

Hours of loneliness in the house
without the cry of a child,
or the pride of being parents.

That was Elizabeth and Zechariah.
All of us have our hopes, longings,
and all of us have had to accept what is not to be.

A marriage that didn't work out
or a relationship that broke up,
a promotion not offered
or an exam not passed,
good health not restored;
hopes for the recovery of someone dear,
the sudden death of one in the family,
or making things better in a parish,
or a new start for someone in trouble ...

Like an alarm clanging in a derelict building,
our disappointment echoes to God
from the depths of our soul.

God hears,
God listens,
God offers,

not the magic of a Christmas Santa-present,
but the love, hope and inner strength
that doesn't make our disappointment
all-embracing and total.

Come, Lord Jesus,
child of hope;
come, Lord Jesus,
child of light;
come Lord Jesus,
child of God.

REFLECTION

Some disappointment in life comes from placing our hopes in the wrong place. Like trying to be musical when we are tone-deaf, trying for exam results that are beyond our IQ, looking for a promotion which is outside our capabilities. Other disappointments are caused by others, and are of a different type, because they lead to frustration and anger about something we cannot influence. No matter where they come from, disappointments are part and parcel of life. If we ignore them, they catch up on us, making us cynical and angry. There are also disappointments from our idealism and trying to do good. Can we bring all our disappointments to God, let out the feelings of disappointment to him, accept them fully, forgive ourselves and others if need be, and then let hope and light heal our wounded desires and inspire us to keep walking that step farther and farther into the love of the Christ-child?

1.4   Loneliness

INTRODUCTION Loneliness is an experience in everyone's life, at different times. It is a wilderness time, when you can feel lost or depressed; one of the worst feelings a person has.

SCRIPTURE *Jesus desires the company of his friends in his Passion.*

They went to a place called Gethsemane, and he said to his disciples, 'Sit here while I pray' ... He took with him Peter, James and John, and began to be distressed and agitated. And he said to them, 'I am deeply grieved, even to death; remain here and keep awake' ... He came and found them sleeping; and he said to Peter, 'Simon are you asleep? Could you not keep awake one hour?' *Mark 14:32-37.*

PSALM
My God, my God, why have you forsaken me?
You are far from my plea and the cry of my distress.
O my God, I call by day and you give no reply,
I call by night and I find no peace. *Psalm 22.*

PRAYER
Loneliness is like
a well gone dry
a misty winter's day,
fruit dry of its juice.

It's the child lost in the store,
the teenager without friends,
the adult alone in the crowd,
the old person alone with memories.

It's an experience at every age,
a fierce feeling sometimes,
and can lead to despair.
And Jesus was lonely,
in his agony in the garden
when friends slept through his need.

In the darkness of loneliness
is found the hand of God.
For in loneliness as in friendship
we come close to the love of God.

Child of Mary and Joseph,
child of their home,
give peace to my loneliness;
come child of God,
in loneliness may I find you,
friend in aloneness.

REFLECTION

A splendid poster reminds us of a central truth at the heart of the human experience of loneliness. A father holds his daughter on his shoulders as they gaze together at a vast ocean. Beneath the picture are the words: 'We ask God for answers and God sends us a person to help us live with the questions.' That person, finally, is Jesus, but God also comes to us incarnate in many others. We are not alone, but each of us often feels that way. As we wrestle with the tensions between our need to be with others, and our need to be alone, especially in the middle of our lives, we will feel acutely that deep and existential loneliness that is so much a part of the human condition.

L Patrick Carroll and Katherine Dyckman, *Chaos or Creation.*

1.5 Mourning

INTRODUCTION Mourning a loss is to dwell in the wilderness. The loss of a loved one, a relationship, a friend, is a loss of something in oneself. And you look for comfort, for help, for fulness again.

SCRIPTURE *Mary mourned her son at the cross; a woman of strength and sorrow; one who consoles us in our mourning.*

Standing close to Jesus' cross were his mother, his mother's sister, Mary, the wife of Clopas, and Mary Magdalene. Jesus saw his mother and the disciple he loved standing there; so he said to his mother, 'He is your son'.

Then he said to the disciple, 'She is your mother.' From that time the disciple took her to live in his home. *John 19:25-27.*

PSALM
Turn to me, O Lord, and be gracious;
give me your strength;
save the child of your serving girl.
Show me a sign of your favour;
you, O Lord, are my comforter, my help. *Psalm 85.*

PRAYER
I mourned the death of a father;
gone was the one I held so special,
gone was the one who held me so special;
held as a baby in arms,
held in the heart in love.

There's a gap in the family;
a chair that will always be empty;
and nobody will sing the song the way he did.

Mourning is lonely, even when shared;
it has desolate colours and discordant tones.
And you wonder, when will it pass?

Never and always, is the answer.
And what gives hope?
Somewhere in the midst of suffering prayer,
I sensed the voice of Jesus,
'I know how you feel,
I lost my father too'.

And then I knew what compassion was,
though the loss was still sore,
though the chair was still empty
though the song would no more be sung.
But I wasn't alone.

Lord, child of comfort,
be my comforter in mourning;
be close to all who mourn,
child of Christmas,
child of Mary.

REFLECTION

The Paschal mystery of the death and resurrection of Christ is the centre-piece of Christian hope. It is here that the peculiar character of Christian hope emerges. By including specific reference to the cross of Christ, Christian hope recognises that suffering and death are an intrinsic part of Christian existence. No amount of talk about the resurrection can remove the stark realities of suffering and death. Instead

Christian hope resides in the crucified Christ, acknowledging that this historical reality embraces both darkness and light, tragedy and transformation, sadness and joy, death and resurrection. To this extent it must be said without qualification that the shape of Christian hope is cruciform, made up of a bright darkness. Darkness, as it were, becomes a special kind of light within Christian hope.

Dermot Lane, *In Search of Hope.*

1.6   Wilderness of guilt

INTRODUCTION There is the wilderness of guilt; feelings of wishing things hadn't happened, sorrow at hurt we've caused, regret at the good we didn't do. We know we need the cleansing of God's forgiveness. And God is joyful in forgiveness.

SCRIPTURE *A short piece from the story of the prodigal son depicts the father waiting in forgiveness for his son, like God for you.*

'But when he came to himself, the younger son said, 'I will get up and go to my father, and I will say to him, 'Father, I am no longer worthy to be called your son: treat me as one of your hired hands.' So he got up and went to his father. But while he was still far off, his father saw him and was filled with compassion; he ran and put his arms around him and kissed him. *Luke 15:17-20.*

PSALM
Sin speaks to sinners
in the depths of the heart.
There is no fear of God
before their eyes.

Your love, Lord, reaches to the heavens;
your truth to the skies.
Your justice is like God's mountain,
your judgements like the deep. *Psalm 35.*

PRAYER

'Please God, get rid of this awful guilt' –
a prayer many of us make.
Guilt is like a blot on an artist's canvas,
for we are God's work of art,
and God is working on us,
drawing us into fuller love,
etching traces of his love into our whole being.

And guilt can block our enjoyment of who we are.

Guilt is like remorse, like shame, like self-hatred;
and like those feelings it is unproductive.
All it means is that we feel bad over something we've done.

And we can't unscramble eggs nor turn the clock back;
we can only admit our wrong-doing,
and put it where all the past belongs:
in the hands of our loving God.

Lord Jesus, may the salvation of your birth
free me from guilt;
may your love at Christmas
forgive me my sin.

Come among us,
child of peace,
child of forgiveness,
child of Mary,
Word made flesh.

Some of us like change,
others like to stay put.
Change can be threatening,
like storm clouds nearing the climber:

the change from home to a flat,
from school to college or a job,
from single to married life,
from an unhappy marriage to single life again,
from bitterness to forgiveness,
from conflict to understanding,

and changes we don't ask for:
bereavement,unemployment,illness,death.

In the many ways we experience change,
are we not sometimes afraid?

The change of the gospel of Jesus
is to change for the better in love;
we are called to go a step farther in love like his.

Jesus, child of change, Lord of the future,
let me know that all good change in your name,
the change from sin to love, selfishness to openness,
is a change in the power of love.
And where there is love, I find you.

REFLECTION
Above all, trust in the slow work of God. We are, quite natur-
ally, impatient in everything to reach the end without delay.
We should like to skip the intermediate stages.We are impatient of being on the way to something unknown, something new. And yet it is the law of all progress that it is made
by passing through some stages of instability – and that it
may take a very long time.

And so I think it is with you. Your ideas mature gradually – let them grow. Let them shape themselves without undue haste. Don't try to force them on, as though you could be today what time (that is to say, grace and circumstances acting on your own good will) will make you to-morrow.

Only God could say what this new spirit gradually forming within you shall be. Give our Lord the benefit of believing that his hand is guiding you, and accept the anxiety of feeling yourself in suspense and incomplete.

Teilhard de Chardin SJ

2.2   Self-blame to self-acceptance

INTRODUCTION None of us can live without forgiveness, but very often the first step to believing in the forgiveness of God – or of another – is to forgive ourselves. This is a conversion: from self-blame to forgiving and accepting oneself.

SCRIPTURE *Forgiving yourself is a grace which comes from believing you are forgiven by God. Jesus spoke a lot about the forgiveness of God and offered the gift of that forgiveness; and it was promised from before his birth, in the prayer of Zechariah for his son, John the Baptist.*

You, child, will go before the Lord, to prepare his ways,
to give knowledge of salvation to his people
by the forgiveness of their sins.
By the tender mercy of our God,
the dawn from on high will break upon us. *Luke 1:76-78.*

PSALM
My sin is always before me,
against you, you alone, have I sinned,
what is evil in your sight I have done.
Give me again the joy of your help,
do not deprive me of your holy Spirit. *Psalm 51.*

PRAYER
Can I forgive myself?
The times when I look back on life
and it's like a lovely canvas
with one blot in the corner –
and all I see is the blot?

All of us have rooms in the heart
which seem to contain
within our own view
all the meanness and badness of our lives.
And then there's shame and guilt,
and the disbelief that God is forgiving,
and we fail to see the beauty of ourselves.

Allow the past be received into the mercy of God,
for that is where it belongs.
The hands of God in Jesus Christ
wounded for love and forgiveness,
are gentle and kind enough to hold all my sins,
all the memories which bring on guilt;
for the hands of God in Jesus Christ
were nailed to a cross of forgiveness.

Every memory that holds back forgiveness
is like a dark shadow over me;
can I allow the light of the Christ-child,
begin the flow of forgiveness?

Lord, help me forgive myself,
as you, the child of forgiveness,
have forgiven me.

REFLECTION
What the world needs first of all, and most of all, from the
Church, is comfort, help in lifting and understanding its
pain, its wounds, its anxieties, its raging restlessness, its
temptations, its infidelities and its sin. Like the prodigal son,
it needs first of all to be surprised by unconditional love.
Some time later, and there will be time for that, it will want
some challenge. And our comfort must be offered not on the

basis of human optimism, human forgiveness, and human potential; in some respects, the world already understands more deeply than we do. No, the comfort that we offer is that which we ourselves will first feel when we begin to realise how deep, wide, all-embracing and all-forgiving is the heart of God.

Ronald Rolheiser, *Give Comfort to My People*

2.3   From greed to sharing

INTRODUCTION John the Baptist refers to greed in his sermons. Advent is a call to us to share equally, to live justly and to centre our concerns not only on ourselves but on others too.

SCRIPTURE *John's sermon is strong, yet founded on good principles of justice.*

And the crowds asked John, 'What then should we do?' In reply he said to them, 'Whoever has two coats must share with anyone who has none; and whoever has food must do likewise.' Even tax collectors came to be baptised and they asked him, 'Teacher, what should we do?' He said to them, 'Collect no more than the amount prescribed for you.' Soldiers also asked him, 'And we, what should we do?' He said to them, 'Do not extort money from anyone by threats or false accusation, and be satisfied with your wages.'
Luke 3:10-14.

PSALM
May the mountains bring forth peace for the people
and the hills, justice.
May he defend the poor of the people,
and save the children of the needy.
He shall endure like the sun and the moon,
he shall descend like rain on the meadow,
like raindrops on the earth. *Psalm 71.*

PRAYER

Strong are our desires to collect, to hoard
and to have more;
in individuals and in groups,
and in nations.

The word of God speaks against this urge.
God's word is a strong invitation
to give away surplus and share our wealth.

It's an age-old challenge,
but always new
because greed is ever young.

Why should I share?
Why should a country share?
Why is the problem still there?

Why is it that in ten years
the best paid salaries have increased by over 50%
and the welfare payments by only 19%?

Convert us, Lord,
guide us in the new direction
of equality,
in the home, the country
and in the whole world.

Come, Lord Jesus,
urgent for justice,
urgent for equality,
child of God.

REFLECTION

Prayer opens us to the world. To the city or neighbourhood we live in, and to the people we are close to. And especially to their cries: real prayer involves us with the homeless and the hungry, the poor and the unfree. It involves us much with the suffering that is caused by injustice. Prayer that cushions us from the person waiting for months on a hospital bed, or from young people unemployed because of where they come from, or from the woman with no legal aid in court, or such realities, is soft prayer. Our prayer 'Come quickly, Lord Jesus' is into this darkness of injustice. An urgent desire for justice comes to birth through real prayer. A prayer which winces and asks 'does it have to be like this?' and which struggles and says, 'it cannot be like this'. Real prayer is a welcome from Jesus into his heart, and his heart is the heart that longs and yearns for justice. Little wonder that Mary praised God for filling the hungry with good things, for the God of justice was coming to birth within her.

2.4   Bitterness to freedom

INTRODUCTION Our bitterness calls from within us for conversion. Part of everyone's life, it's like a cancer of the soul if it's not moved. And only love of others and of God, can do this.

SCRIPTURE *Jesus' words to leave a gift at the altar if there is bitterness in the heart is a call to a change of heart.*

So when you are offering your gift at the altar, if you remember that your brother or sister has something against you, leave your gift here before the altar and go; first, be reconciled to your brother or sister, and then come back and offer your gift. *Matthew 5:23-24.*

PSALM
We heard with our own ears Lord,
our ancestors have told us the story
of the things you did in their days,
you yourself, in days long ago...
It was your right hand, your arm,
and the light of your face, for you loved them.
Stand up and come to our help.
Redeem us because of your love. *Psalm 43.*

PRAYER
There are places in each human heart
where bitterness finds a home.
It is only human to feel bitter at times
at how you were treated by a friend,

a child, a spouse, a neighbour,
and bitter at how life has treated you.

And that room can become bigger,
as it houses more and more bitterness,
and with it pain and grief.

It is not wrong to feel bitter,
but it is sad to let that bitterness grow.
Then the heart
festers, and becomes cold,
the root-place of all complaints.

The call of Jesus is to let compassion grow,
to make space in the heart for understanding and love,
to allow even forgiveness and warmth
join hands with coldness and grief.

It is hard:
the bitterness of years -
of abuse at the hands of others,
at their greed and injustice
is not quickly changed.

But it can change
with time and prayer.
The healing grace of Jesus
can touch the bitter spaces of the heart;
and I ask that this may be.

Lord, may I make the step
a day at a time
from bitterness to warmth,
from grudges to freedom,
from sadness at my lot to love.

Forgive us our sins,
as we forgive those who sin against us.

REFLECTION

Two cousins said they don't know why they don't speak to each other. Something happened a long time ago between their parents, and the families have been bitter ever since. Bitterness happens over land and money, over the favourite in a family and the neglected child, over the spouse who was unfaithful and a neglectful child. And there are always reasons for bitterness. Some bitterness is well-grounded: the abuse of a child is one that comes to mind. Bitterness takes up space in the heart and the heart needs its space for growth and love. But it can be replaced. Not forgotten, but replaced. By understanding others and why they act as they do, by the healing power of time, by a knowledge that nobody is perfect. No matter what, no matter how deep and well-deserved the bitterness, it damages the one who suffers it. It is healed also by the healing grace of Jesus; his love from the bitter wood of the Cross can be a starting-point to emptying the heart of bitterness so that the love of Jesus may make its home within us in the desire to be free and to forgive. Ask strongly for that healing for in it is true freedom of the soul.

INTRODUCTION One of the calls to true Christian conversion is to value justice, and to desire a world where justice reigns, pray for this justice and work for it.

SCRIPTURE *Mary's prayer of praise includes a call to justice.*
And Mary said...
He has brought down the powerful from their thrones,
and lifted up the lowly.
He has filled the hungry with good things,
and sent the rich empty away. *Luke 1:52-53.*

PSALM
As for me, I will always hope
and praise you more and more.
My lips will tell of your justice
and day by day of your help
though I can never tell it all.
I will declare the Lord's mighty deeds
proclaiming your justice, your's alone. *Psalm 70.*

PRAYER
Lord Jesus, open our minds to the truth
of the world around us:
let us be brave enough to admit
that huge inequalities exist between us:
between people of our own city,
and between different parts of the world.

Lord Jesus, open our hearts to the suffering
of the world around us;
let us be compassionate enough to admit
that millions just barely exist
while other millions have too much.

Lord Jesus, open our hands to give from what we have
to those who have not even enough;
let us be generous in sharing with those in need
what we have received;
for when we give, you give through us,
and when we give, we give to you.

Draw us into that circle of love,
the love of heaven reaching the love of earth,
the love that calls for justice,
the love that does justice.

Come, Lord Jesus, child of justice;
awaken in us a desire for equality,
for compassion, for justice.

REFLECTION

On this night, as we Christians have done every year for 20
centuries, we recall that God's reign is now in the world and
that Christ has inaugurated the fulness of time. His birth at-
tests that God is now marching with us in history, that we do
not go alone, and that our aspiration for peace, for justice,
for a reign of divine law, for something holy, is far from
earth's realities. We can hope for it, not because we humans
are able to construct that realm of happiness which God's
holy words proclaim, but because the builder of a reign of
justice, of love and of peace is already in the midst of us.

Oscar Romero

2.6   From prejudice to tolerance

INTRODUCTION The salvation and love of God is universal and challenges us to grow out of narrow prejudices about people and classes of people. We are all equal in the sight of God.

SCRIPTURE *In the temple one day, people saw only a child and poor parents, but Simeon saw the son of God. Can we see beyond and within each person to the life and love of God within them?*

Guided by the Spirit, Simeon came into the temple ... he took the child in his arms and praised God, saying,
'Master ...
my eyes have seen your salvation,
which you have prepared in the presence of all peoples,
a light for the revelation of the Gentiles,
and for the glory of your people Israel.'
And the child's mother and father were amazed at what was being said about him. *Luke 2:27-33.*

PSALM
Preserve me, God, I take refuge in you.
I say to the Lord: 'You are my God.
My happiness lies in you alone.'
He has put into my heart a marvellous love
for the faithful ones who dwell in his land.
You will show me the path of life,
the fulness of joy in your presence,
at your right hand happiness for ever. *Psalm 16.*

PRAYER

The boy behind the counter had spiked hair,
and looked way-out, a bit weird.
A customer was heard saying,
'He was very kind for that type of person'.
The reaction is understandable,
but none the less sad for its frequency.
The outside of a person may hide goodness or evil within,
and the labels we see on people hide their uniqueness.

There is safety in prejudice,
for if you can be sure of your judgement
about Catholics and Anglicans,
Presbyterians and Methodists,
about black and white, poor and rich, young and old,
then you need not be touched
by the goodness and the needs of others.

Hunger is no less painful when you are poor,
and poverty no less hurtful if you have once been rich.
Human feelings of joy and sadness have few distinctions.

And the one distinction not made in God's heart
is between people:
his love is unconditional,
without favourites,
except that he has a special care
for people who are down and harshly treated by others.

Lord, I ask for
the eyes to see each other as you see us,
the ears to hear each other as you hear,
the heart to feel for each other as you love.

Come, Lord Jesus.

REFLECTION

What do you need for the unprejudiced eye? For the eye that sees someone as Jesus does? His insight into people was that they were immensely loved by God. And he knew that he himself was loved too. Prejudice comes from a harsh attitude to others because they are different from myself. And sometimes from insecurity in myself. Groups fear each other. But there is also knowledge. We need to get rid of notions that one nation is mean and another is drunk; that one group of people is unfaithful and another is greedy. People are individual and unique. We have common traits with our nation and our class, but we are not defined by that. The Christmas crib is for everyone: low enough that we have to stoop to get into it, and humble enough to get rid of pretensions. And the child in the crib is multi-coloured, belonging to the whole human race and to God. That means he belongs everywhere, that each of us belongs in the heart of God too, and that we belong in the whole world.

The third week of Advent

Witness

3.1   The Baptist

INTRODUCTION The main preoccupation of John's life was to prepare the way for God: to 'decrease' while Jesus 'increased' in his influence. He saw himself as the light showing another light, Jesus, the light of the world.

SCRIPTURE *John's identity in life was totally caught up in his relationship with God in Jesus.*

There was a man sent from God whose name was John. He came as a witness to testify to the light, so that all might believe through him. He himself was not the light, but he came to testify to the light, the true light, which enlightens everyone, was coming into the world. *John 1:6-9.*

PSALM
It is you, O Lord, who are my hope,
my trust, O Lord, since my youth.
On you I have leaned from my birth,
from my mother's womb you have been my help. *Psalm 70.*

PRAYER
I wonder how did John testify to the light;
how did he live so that people looked for God in him?

The words he spoke – did their urgency move people to God?
Or a brightness in the eyes
we sometimes see with holy people?

Or maybe his life:
he was a man of honesty in his religion,

who spoke his mind even when opposed,
and who lived what he believed,
and died for his convictions.

We testify to the light of God
in how we live;
in the moments when love shines through us
and when compassion is flowing from us;
the times when people put themselves out for another,
or speak the truth as we know it to be,
and when we give time in prayer.

Maybe that's how we are baptists;
baptising not just with water
but with our personal grace:
baptising with forgiveness of wrongs,
with compassion for the heartache of another,
with love especially for the troubled,
with an urgent concern for the injustices of our times.

Lord Jesus, may my life testify
that love and faith and hope exist,
that equality and justice are at the centre of the gospel,
and that you are present among us.

Come, Lord Jesus, among us and within us.
Come, announced by the Baptist,
come, announced in the life of your people.

REFLECTION
The voices of the Baptist are many today: voices crying for
the poor, voices suggesting a change of the ways we live, a
voice for the priority of mystery and love among us. If you
met John the Baptist, you would have come away a bit different from the meeting, like when people meet a truly good

person. For John was a man rooted totally in God. He lived out of a vision he knew within his heart: a vision of equality and of honesty, of prayer and of truth, which would later lead to martyrdom. John is a witness of God, a witness of the coming of the Lord Jesus, because he knew from within his own personality the human being's need for God and the emptiness of the world looking for the fulness of God.

Genuine faith is stretched in life,
for many of life's experiences stretch our faith –
the loneliness and the sadnesses of life,
its harsh dealings to good people,
its cruelty to innocent children,
its unfairness and inequality.
And faith is about things unseen,
when what seems natural certainty is tested.
Faith, even when confused, gets strong in testing;
and Joseph is a patron of confusion.

In his confusion he did not rebel:
he searched for the truth
and was willing to allow that his own opinion
might be wrong.

The testing of faith is always for the growth of faith.
Don't we expect faith to grow easily and sunnily;
but it never grows or deepens without testing,
as any plant strains to grow.

Lord, when my faith is stretched
by the world or people around me,
or by the way life deals itself to me,
help me to know that it can grow
and become stronger.

Come, Lord Jesus,
come to us in faith;
come to us in unbelief.

I believe, help my unbelief.

REFLECTION

'If you don't bring God to church, you won't find him there', goes an old saying. And it points at the essential link of life and faith. Behind every faith question is a human question; maybe a human hurt or pain. People have started to talk about faith and ended up talking about a weakening marriage or a sick child. Or wondering about a decision or if they should change a job. Faith questions are seldom simply only faith. And we need the honesty to face both the faith and what we see as the human side of our lives. We can complain about faith, but our complaint can be a very human denial of our loneliness or our disillusion with a friend. Faith is of the heart and the heart is human. Joseph's questions to God had to do with God's faithfulness to him, but it also had to do with the huge and important decision of his engagement to Mary. When he didn't separate them he was able to feel the presence of God and know what was God's will for him.

3.4   The shepherds

INTRODUCTION The shepherds were witnesses of Christmas; in their own simplicity they believed the word of God through the angels, that a Saviour had been born. We are witnesses to the coming of the Saviour in our own poverty and weakness.

SCRIPTURE *The first guests to the birth of Christ were among the poorest of people. Jesus' later life would show that his favourites are the poor.*

When the angels had left them and gone into heaven, the shepherds said to one another, 'Let us go now to Bethlehem and see this thing that has taken place, which the Lord has made known to us.' So they went with haste and found Mary and Joseph, and the child lying in the manger ... The shepherds returned, glorifying and praising God for all they had heard and seen, as it had been told them. *Luke 2:15-18.*

PSALM
For God has never despised
nor scorned the poverty of the poor.
From the poor he has not hidden his face,
but he heard the poor when they cried. *Psalm 21.*

PRAYER
The ones whom nobody expected:
these were the shepherds who visited the crib.
Poor, despised, lowly,
names later given to Jesus;
like has recognised like.

For he had emptied himself willingly
to be in solidarity with those
who feel emptiest and poorest in our eyes.

The shepherds felt at home with Mary and Joseph
because Mary and Joseph felt at home among the poor.
Jesus had come to his own,
and of his own,
only these welcomed him.

When you are poor –
poor in body and in possessions,
poor in strength and health,
poor in soul and sin,
then you are close to the shepherds,
and when you are at your poorest,
you are at God's doorway,
for God loves you most
when you love yourself least.

Lord Jesus, may my own poverty
open my heart to poverty more urgent than mine.
Come, child of poverty,
child of simplicity,
child who was outcast,
come, Lord Jesus.

REFLECTION
Pretensions about our dignity keep us from knowing God.
Pretensions about our value and our wealth keep us from
being open to the song of angels in life and in death. Those
who are humble in heart, mind and body know the real
meaning of Christmas, and are real witnesses to Christmas.
Humble in body means enjoying the body God has given
you, and accepting how you look. The consumerism of the

Who knows what's ahead?

Parents wonder will they be able for parenting,
and the world will offer such mixtures to a child:
love and danger, use and abuse, health and illness.
Zechariah and Elizabeth hoped, as every parent hopes,
for the best for their little son,
for good health, love, happiness.

They sensed he was destined for something great
with all the words of God about him;
what would they have thought if they knew
that their son would be martyred,
for speaking the truth?
And they would be glad that their son
would announce the coming of Christ.

May we rejoice always in the goodness of another's life,
as Mary, Elizabeth, Zechariah,
and later Jesus himself
rejoiced in the honest goodness of John the Baptist.

Come, Lord
announced by the Baptist,
come, cousin, nephew,
son of God,
in our human family.

REFLECTION

What is prayer? Prayer is whatever unites us with God, brings us to an awareness of God, to a love of God, to a longing for God, to surrender to God. That is prayer. Whatever makes us aware of how far we are from God is also a form of prayer. It is real. For example, you are angry with God. You feel alienated with regard to all things spiritual. Yet, somehow, somewhere within your being, you are still seeking God. In this whole process there is a movement of prayer.

Prayer is building a relationship with God. We build it whenever we are in touch with who we are before God. We want to be real. We want to know the real God. We question the truth and sincerity of our longings. We are willing to take steps to develop that relationship no matter what the cost. We are in earnest therefore about trying to build that relationship with God. This is prayer.

Kathleen O'Sullivan, *Light Out of Darkness*.

3.6   The Magi

INTRODUCTION Following some sort of an intuition in their lives, the Magi in the gospel story search for Jesus' birth-place, and are representatives of everyone's search for truth and for God.

SCRIPTURE *The search of the Magi in the gospel is presented as the search of the Gentiles for Jesus; the Magi of the story represent all pilgrims on the way to Jesus Christ.*

Some wise men from the East came to Jerusalem, asking 'Where is the child who has been born King of the Jews?' ... When they had heard the king, they set out; and there, ahead of them went the star that they had seen at its rising, until it stopped over the place where the child was...When they saw that the star had stopped, they were overwhelmed with joy.
Matthew 2:1-10

PSALM
O God, give your judgement to the king,
to a king's son your justice,
that he may judge your people in justice,
and your poor in right judgement.

In his days justice shall flourish,
and peace till the moon fails. *Psalm 71.*

PRAYER
Think of them on their journey,
a journey to Bethlehem,
like our journey to Christmas.

Seekers of truth,

for the One who is himself
the Truth of God.

Searching through stars
for the One through whom all stars and light were made.
Travelling a path unknown
to the One whose path was being prepared
and who would call himself the Way.

Burdened with gifts
and the best gift they would encounter
was the gift of God to them.

Did they pray on the way?
Did they wonder on the journey?
Did they feel like turning back?

In all this, aren't they just like the rest of us?
And aren't we just like them,
men and women on the path to God,
Magi ourselves because we search for the pathway of truth?

Lord, child of wisdom and knowledge,
let us know that the fullest wisdom in life
is the wisdom of putting on the mind of God.

REFLECTION
Now as at all times I can see in the mind's eye,
In their stiff, painted clothes, the pale unsatisfied ones
Appear and disappear in the blue depth of the sky
With all their ancient faces like rain-beaten stones,
And all their helms of silver hovering side by side,
And all their eyes still fixed, hoping to find once more,
Being by Calvary's turbulence unsatisfied,
The uncontrollable mystery on the bestial floor.

W B Yeats, *The Magi.*

The fourth week of Advent

Birth

4.1   The birth of God

INTRODUCTION As a new birth is a new life on earth, the Christmas birth of Jesus is a new presence of God among us. Simple, ordinary, and for all time. God is making his home with us.

SCRIPTURE
No one has ever seen God. It is God the only Son, who is close to the Father's heart, who has made him known.
John 1:18.

PSALM
How gracious is the Lord and just;
our God has compassion.
The Lord protects the simple hearts;
I was helpless so he saved me. *Psalm 114.*

PRAYER
In the simplicity of Bethlehem God is born;
in the manger is the God of eternity.
The word of God is sung by angels,
and more surprising, is heard by the poor.

God is born:
in the flesh of a child,
in the love of Mary,
in the care of Joseph,
in the hospitality of Elizabeth and Zechariah,
in the journey of the shepherds,
in the heart of the Magi.

Our Christmas concern for each other
is a reflection of what is happening
in the heart of God.

It is the birth of God,
a new birth of love, compassion,
justice, reconciliation and peace.

For what happens at Christmas
is that the heart of God in his Son,
has become close to humanity's heart:
they have become one.
In a new way God and humanity
are not separated;
and all because this child is born.

Come, Lord Jesus,
God of heaven,
Child of earth,
be born, soon among us,
God made flesh!

REFLECTION

Can you look at the Child of Christmas and see God? If you can, then you can look at everyone around Christmas and see a child of God.

Everyone belongs in the crib: whatever the label ... alcoholic, gambler, gay, old, young, black, white, travellers, especially victims of prejudice ... all in the crib.

See your family like this and pray for them; see your friends like this and pray for them; and your enemies, people you don't like; see them in the crib of Bethlehem and pray for them.

Then we see with the eyes of Jesus.

4.2   Gentle his birth

INTRODUCTION The birth of Jesus is surrounded by gentleness: gentle easing of people's fears, gentle preparations for birth, gentle invitations of people who come to visit him. Gentleness is the mark of those who receive him; only the unbelievers and the fearful receive him with fear and violence.

SCRIPTURE *Jesus himself calls out his gentleness as a reason we would come to him and follow him.*

Come to me, all you that are weary and are carrying heavy burdens, and I will give you rest. Take my yoke upon you, and learn from me, for I am gentle and humble in heart, and you will find rest for your souls. For my yoke is easy and my burden is light. *Matthew 11:28-30.*

PSALM
O Lord, my heart is not proud,
nor haughty my eyes.
I have not gone after things too great
nor marvels beyond me.
Truly I have set my soul
in silence and peace.
As a child has rest in a mother's arms,
even so my soul. *Psalm 130.*

PRAYER
With gentleness he came into our world,
with peace for his people and his friends,
and with a desire for the good of his people.

In the gentle rain which waters the earth,
God comes among us.
In the gentle breeze which cools our heat,
the Lord is near.
In the gentle soil which welcomes our seeds,
the Spirit moves.

In the gentle touch of compassion and care,
Jesus is near.
In the gentle word of consolation and cheer,
the voice of God is heard.
In the love that makes us gentle,
the Word is made flesh.

In the gentleness that was strong,
in the love that was faithful,
in the birth that recalls us to death,
the Lord has come among us – God is with us.

Glory and praise to you, gentle God.
Kindly child of God in heaven,
one of us on earth,
God, now and forever.

REFLECTION
The God of Christmas is a gentle God. The child born of Mary
doesn't look pompous or important or self-centred. He hasn't
all the answers. He was born as a poor child, not in the trap-
pings of royalty, politics or the church. He kept this gentleness all his life. Is this our view of God? We may pick up early
in life that God loves us if we're good, or worse still, only
when we're perfect. But God loves each of us because we are
who we are. Let God's all-seeing eye (an image often used to
catch us out) wink at you! Maybe a desire for perfection pre-

vents us knowing God is gentle and prevents us being gentle on ourselves. Or guilt for sins we have never forgiven ourselves for. Or maybe we're not too gentle ourselves: we want control and power, or we rail at the injustices of the world. We need to allow God look after the world, as the sun sets each day without our help, or we need to accept that God looks at the love in a person's heart rather than achievements. Christmas is the birth of the gentle God. The God who loves you – all of you. Not just the nice side of you, but totally, loving you most where you love yourself least. Give space for the gentle God to smile at you this Christmas, touch you, speak to you. 'Blessed the gentle,' said Jesus, 'for they shall inherit the earth.' He could say that because he grew to maturity in the gentleness of the home of Mary and Joseph, and he knew from his own life the joy and beauty of the gentle.

* * *

It is not you that shapes God; God shapes you. You are the work of God. Await the hand of the artist who does all things in due season. Offer God your heart, soft and pliable; and keep the form in which the artist has fashioned you. Let your clay be moist lest you grow hard and lose the imprint of God's fingers.

St Irenaeus

4.3   The birth of joy

INTRODUCTION There is a quiet joy in the home of Bethlehem; a joy not of comfort but of love, not of wealth but of
simplicity, not of individualism but of shared purpose. It was
a joy that lasted for Jesus and Mary and Joseph through the
future.

SCRIPTURE *The joy of Jesus and a life of love are intimately
linked.*
I have told you this,
so that my own joy may be in you,
and your joy be complete.
This is my commandment,
love one another
as I have loved you. *John 15:11-12.*

PSALM
Many keep saying, 'Who will put happiness before our eyes?'
Let the light of your face shine on us.
Lord, to my heart you are a richer joy
than all their corn and new wine.
In peace I lie down and at once fall asleep,
for it is you, and none other, Lord,
who make me rest secure.

PRAYER
Mary, young mother,
you prayed your song of joy;
your song that God had graced you
with love and with motherhood.

It was a joy that came from an open heart:
and a personality fully open to God.
Your openness shared the fragrance of an open flower
and your welcome to God danced like wheat in the sun.

Your joy was shared:
joy of pregnancy as you waited for Jesus,
joy of love of Joseph,
joy of friendship with Elizabeth.

Isn't the joy of Christmas always a shared joy?
The song of angels,
the visit of shepherds,
and a prayer of thanks and praise
composed with your friend Elizabeth.

Is there any joy that is not shared?

Come, child of heaven's joy,
come, child of earth's warmth,
come, child of Mary.
Come, share our joy,
let us share in your risen joy.

REFLECTION

We will comfort the world, and it will be comforted, when we show it that God sees its heart with the eyes of the heart, that God feels for it more than it feels for itself, that God never feels frightened or wronged by the assertions of its freedom, that God is not put off by all the times we turn our back on what we know is best, that God empathises with our lusts, our greed, our anger, our jealousies and our failures, that God never stops loving us for a moment even when we put ourselves in hell. And that God stands in the middle of our huddled, shivering, timid, wounded, and guilty hearts and breathes out peace. We will comfort the world when we tell it that, in spite of everything, its life is good. The world will be finally helped by us when we trust God enough to have the courage to tell it to live, even to risk mistakes, because in the end, all will be well, and all will be well and every manner of being will be well.

Ronald Rolheiser, *Give Comfort to My People*.

4.4 The birth of truth

INTRODUCTION The gospel is the word of God giving the true meaning to human life; the gospel of the Christ-child guides us in the way of finding meaning and all truth in life.

SCRIPTURE
In the beginning was the Word, and the Word was with God and the Word was God ... And the Word became flesh and lived among us, and we have seen his glory, the glory as of a father's only son, full of grace and truth. *John 1:14.*

PSALM
The Lord is good and upright.
He shows the path to those who stray,
He guides the humble in the right path;
He teaches his way to the poor. *Psalm 24.*

PRAYER
In the questions of life,
we look for the truth,
and search for the true meaning of life.
A boy and a girl in love
want the truth from each other.
And there are big questions we ask
about eternity and God and birth.

Where did I come from?
Where am I going?
What am I here for?
Jesus, what have you to say to these questions?

You come from God,

and you go to God:
this is the truth
of the origins and destiny of human life;
we come from love and we go to love.
And more than that:
Love is with us on all of life's journey,
for God makes his home in each of us.
The human mind wants truth
like the human heart wants love
and the human spirit wants eternity.

This is the gift of the God-made-human:
it is a truth to want this and to yearn for it,
and a truth that we can reach our fulfilment,
like a river reaches the sea,
and starlight reaches our planet.

Come, Lord Jesus, God of truth, child of truth;
lead me through the wide searching of my mind
into your eternal truth.

REFLECTION
In the beginning was the dream and the dream was with God
and the dream was God. We are part of God's dream. God
dreams in us. Can you remember your childhood dreams?
Trailing clouds of glory, you were the centre of the world.
You would spread love and joy everywhere; you would
change the face of the earth. Your life would be as happy as
the bright day was long. Are you living your dream now, or
did someone steal it? Or did it die? ... We weep at the dis-
tance between what we now are and what we once dreamed
of becoming. We will recover this dream: it is our first window of wonder.

Donal O'Leary, *Windows of Wonder.*

4.5   The birth of love

INTRODUCTION A new love is born with the birth of Jesus. A love that goes beyond nation, class, age. All-inclusive, total love of God for people; and an invitation to be that love.

SCRIPTURE *The picture of the birth of Jesus can be looked at with the eyes of the heart, with the eyes of love. It is a picture of love: of Mary and Joseph for each other and for Jesus, and of God for us.*

And she gave birth to her first-born son and wrapped him in bands of cloth, because there was no room for them in the inn ... and suddenly there was with the angel a multitude of the heavenly host, praising God and saying, 'Glory to God in the highest heaven, and on earth peace, good will among people'. *Luke 2:7-14.*

PSALM
In the scroll of the book it is written of me,
my delight is to do your will;
your law, my God,
is deep in my heart. *Psalm 40.*

PRAYER
At every birth new love enters the world,
the heart of God has stretched a bit more
and a new incarnation of love is born.

Whether by love of parents, by plan, or by chance,
no matter what the motivation of the parents,
each birth is a new love of God among us;
each child is Emmanuel, God-with-us.

Is that why we spontaneously rejoice at birth?
Vulnerable, tiny, hopeful,
a sense of the miracle –
all the tone of birth.

And this all the more in Bethlehem,
for Jesus was born within the faith of
Mary and Joseph,
and their love of God,
from the love of Father and Spirit.

The world has never been the same since this birth;
let us rejoice, open our hearts
to new love, new hope, new music
in the everlasting song of the angels:

Glory to you, Lord God,
for you are God in the highest heaven,
and you bring this day
peace on earth.

REFLECTION
That then is my theology: I 'know' deep in my guts that the
heart of the eternal God is most wonderfully kind and that
his mercy is infinitely wider than the grey sea which swells
before me as I write. I believe that when we die we are born
into eternal life with God – and that life is what we call heav-
en. If my patients ask me what I believe I tell them. I tell
them that I believe that when we die, not only are we with
God but that we are somehow more alive, more vibrant,
more ourselves than we have ever been before. Just how this
is I do not know – but if life with God is for real, then surely
it's about a fulness of life which is unimaginably wonderful.

Sheila Cassidy, *Light from the Dark Valley.*

There's a lot of love in the gospel story of Jesus' birth. Joseph standing by Mary and Mary growing in love of her son as she carried him and delivered him. There's the care of God in sending angels to bring shepherds to the birth place. And even the care of the inn-keeper who found somewhere for them. And love of the poor: God seemed to look out for the poor as soon as he could. The poor were the first visitors, and the poor were his parents. Birth draws out love in us: a child spontaneously moves us to love and warmth and affection. Birth draws out love also in God. As God was the middle of the heart of the world when Jesus was born, so we are more deeply in the heart of God after the Bethlehem event. And in the heart of God we are in the heart of love, for God is love, and Jesus is the child of love.

4.6   The birth of peace

INTRODUCTION Many promises about the Christ were of peace. Don't we all want peace – in our hearts, homes and world. A heart full of peace spreads peace.

SCRIPTURE *Jesus wants to give peace to his people; it is his wish, and the wish of all of us. May we never tire of wanting peace and hoping for it.*

Peace I leave with you,
my peace I give to you
I do not given to you as the world gives.
Do not let your hearts be troubled,
and do not let them be afraid. *John 14:27.*

PSALM
My heart, be at peace once again,
for the Lord has treated you generously.
He has rescued me from death,
my eyes from tears,
and my feet from stumbling.
I shall pass my life in the presence of the Lord,
in the land of the living. *Psalm 116.*

PRAYER
Please, Lord God, I want peace,
that peace deep within our personality,
and we all search for it.

Not necessarily freedom from all problems,
for many problems are caused by others.
It is a peace no one can take away,
for it is born of God.

Banish fear and give me peace, child of peace;
banish anxiety, and give me peace, mother of peace;
banish worry and give me peace, father of peace,
Mary, Joseph and Jesus,
allow me enter into your environment of peace.

Come, Lord Jesus, soon.
Child of peace,
let me know that I will live
in your peace,
now and forever.
Let me know
your peace within doubts and difficulty.
The peace beyond understanding.

Child of peace, welcome.

REFLECTION
Child do not go
Into the dark places of soul,
For there the grey wolves whine,
The lean grey wolves.

I have been down,
Among the unholy ones who tear
Beauty's white robe and clothe her
In rags of prayer.

Child there is a light somewhere
Under a star,
Sometime it will be for you
A window that looks
Inward to God.

Patrick Kavanagh, *To A Child.*